In the fusion of faith and science, we find,
God's fingerprints, in every design

Dedicated to George and Ese, with lots of love

Copyright © Myrtle Books 2024
Text and illustration © Priscilla Ogboru 2024

All rights reserved. No part of this publication may be reproduced, stored in a retrieval system, or transmitted in any form or by any means, electronic, mechanical, photocopying, recording, or otherwise, without the prior permission of the publisher/author, nor be otherwise circulated in any form of binding or cover other than that in which it is published and without a similar condition being imposed on the subsequent purchaser.

ISBN 978-1-7384931-9-7
www.priscillaogboru.com
All rights reserved.

God's Grand Quest

Written by Priscilla Ogboru
Illustrated by Yevheniia Melnyk

The Creation

In an age before time, in a place far away,
when the world was all night and the stars held no sway,
God sat on a throne, and a smile lit up His face.
He had a bright idea, a plan to put in place.

And so, He said . . .

'I will create something splendid and enormous,
a whole universe vast, endless, and tremendous.
A place of magic and wonder. That it shall be!
There, beautiful creatures will forever be free.'

'It will be splendiferous!' God said.

So with glee, God embarked on this wondrous quest.
This grand vision in His heart, He forged on with zest.
And with every step forward, His quest slowly unfurled.
A tale of mystery and wonder for all the world!

First, He created light, an elemental ray.
Out from Him it came to separate night from day.
Then came the sky, painted different shades of blue
and the clouds, just like cotton, all fluffy and true.

'This is splendiferous,' God said. 'But there is something amiss.'

So He declared, 'Come now, let us add in some ground!'
And promptly, the earth appeared, and spread all around.
He sculpted the mountains and made them tall and grand,
then added valleys and rivers. What a wonderland!

Then the deserts, forests, trees, and all the flowers
emerged from the ground in His creative prowess.
The earth, God coloured in shades of blue, red, and green.
His artistic mastery was charming and pristine!

'This is splendiferous,' God said. 'But still, there is something amiss.'

And so God formed the sun, that bright and blazing sphere,
to light up the day, bringing much warmth and much cheer.
Soon followed the moon, a radiant silver light,
made to shine in the darkness to guide us at night.

In the sky, up on high, God sprinkled twinkling stars.
Balls of gas, big and small, burning bright from afar.
Some were red, some were white; grouped in constellations.
Gazillions of stars in unified formation!

So the planets formed and spun merrily through space,
twirling and whirling in a dance with the sun's rays.
From Mercury to Neptune, they moved in their place.
And the earth's rotation set our clock's moving pace.

'This is splendiferous,' God said. 'But still, there is something amiss.'

In the depths of the ocean, God's vision unfurled.
He made all the sea creatures; they swam and they twirled:
From the tiny clownfish and the enormous blue whale,
to the bell-shaped jellyfish and the spirally snail.

God's creation was really splendid in His sight
He made the dinosaurs, they roamed from morning to night.
Then came a day when the climate changed severely.
Against these changes, the dinosaurs fell, so sadly.

God sighed at the sight but his next idea was most bright. "I will make other animals and create people too, who will rule over everything I have made."

So God made animals: striped, spotted, feathered and furred.
From the bee hummingbird to the albatross bird,
the Etruscan shrew and the giant elephant,
and the lovely swan, all graceful and elegant!

God made all creatures, bright, beautiful, big and small.
The ant, the sloth, the crocodile, and all that crawl.
His creation bloomed and flourished in their clan.
Each with a purpose, a part to play in His plan.

Then He made mankind. Oh, what a glorious sight!
With love and care, He shaped us to be His shining light.
He gave us this world, full of such beauty and grace
and instructed, 'Take care of this marvelous place.'

And then God looked all around and said,
'Now, this is SPLENDIFEROUS!'

Prayer

Dear God, thank you for this beautiful Earth I live on. I am amazed by the mountains, the oceans, the forests, and all the animals that call this place home. Thank you for the sunshine that warms our days and the rain that waters the plants. I see your love in the colours of the flowers and the songs of the birds. Help me to always appreciate the beauty around me and to be grateful for the world you've made. Thank you for giving me this amazing home. Amen!

Our part

So here we are, children of God and Earth's keepers,
free to explore the universe with glee and mirth.
We marvel at nature and its many wonders
and thank God, our Father, for this great universe.

So from the tiny atom to pure elements,
God's scientific process in all is evident.
And in God's quest, so immeasurable and grand,
lies the comforting truth: we are held in His hand!

And that's how it happened, this tale you have been told
about how God made the world, so striking and bold.
Remember to treasure with patience and good care
this immaculate world that we all get to share.

Now listen closely, it is time for you to know
how we can protect the earth, the home that we own.
With little actions big changes we can make,
to preserve God's creation for everyone's sake.

Let us be Earth's friends and its keepers sincere.
With simple actions, let us strive to persevere.
Together, we can work to make a brighter day,
preserving God's splendid creation, come what may!

Prayer

Dear God, thank you for the beautiful Earth you've created. We are grateful for the trees, the flowers, the animals, and all the wonders of nature. Please help us to always appreciate and take care of your creation, just like you take care of us. Help us to remember to be kind to all living creatures and to do our part to keep Earth clean, healthy, and safe. Thank you for always listening to our prayers. Amen!

Everyday actions to protect our earth:

①Turn off all the lights when they are not in use.
Save energy and the planet. There's no excuse!

②Please reduce, reuse, and recycle, my dear.
  Let's keep our earth looked after; keep it clean and clear.

③Now try planting a tree, and let it grow up tall.
It is nature's gift, giving oxygen to all.

4) Save water and use it very wisely, you see
   It is a precious resource for you and for me.

5) Walk or ride a bike whenever you know you can.
   Leave the car parked in the driveway and make a plan.

6) Help keep the oceans clean, free from dirt and debris.
   You'll help marine life to thrive, staying wild and free.

7) Speak up loud and use your voice to help spread the word.
   Tell others how we can all work to help the earth.

Author's note

Thank you so much for purchasing this book and embarking on this journey of creation. If you have enjoyed it, please take a short minute to leave a review and recommend it to a friend.

Visit my website for more information:

www.priscillaogboru.com

Thank you again for your support.

- Priscilla Ogboru

Please click the link or scan the code below to get your free gift

https://priscillaogboru.com/resources/

Other books by author

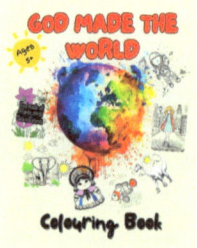

www.ingramcontent.com/pod-product-compliance
Lightning Source LLC
Chambersburg PA
CBHW041527070526
44585CB00003B/117